D1088859

The United States

Colorado

Anne Welsbacher
ABDO & Daughters

visit us at
www.abdopub.com

Published by Abdo & Daughters, 4940 Viking Drive, Suite 622, Edina, Minnesota 55435.
Copyright © 1998 by Abdo Consulting Group, Inc., Pentagon Tower, P.O. Box 36036, Minneapolis, Minnesota 55435 USA. International copyrights reserved in all countries. No part of this book may be reproduced in any form without written permission from the publisher.

Printed in the United States.

Cover and Interior Photo credits: Peter Arnold, Inc., SuperStock

Edited by Julie Berg
Contributing editor Brooke Henderson
Special thanks to our Checkerboard Kids—Tyler Wagner, Francesca Tuminelly, Kenny Abdo

All statistics taken from the 1990 census; The Rand McNally Discovery Atlas of The United States. Other sources: *Colorado*, Fradin, Children's Press, Chicago, 1994; *A Historical Album of Colorado*, Willis, Millbrook Press, Brookfield, 1994; *Colorado*, Bledsoe, Lerner Publications Co., Minneapolis, 1993; America Online, Compton's Living Encyclopedia, 1997; World Book Encyclopedia, 1990.

Library of Congress Cataloging-in-Publication Data

Welsbacher, Anne, 1955-
        Colorado / by Anne Welsbacher.
        p.   cm. -- (The United States)
        Includes index.
        Summary: Surveys the people, geography, and history of the Centennial State.
        ISBN 1-56239-850-4
        1. Colorado--Juvenile literature. [1. Colorado.]   I. Title.   II. Series: United States (Series)
        F776.3.W45   1998
        978.8--dc21   97-5039
                                                                       CIP
                                                                       AC

Contents

Welcome to Colorado

Colorado is the tallest state in the country! It has high mountains. It has deep valleys, gorges, and many rivers. The rivers run through red clay in the land. That made the rivers look red to Spanish explorers. So they named the land Colorado, Spanish for "colored red."

Long ago, Native Americans farmed the land and hunted buffalo. Then Spanish explorers came and brought their horses. Miners found gold in Colorado's mountains. Then many more people came to dig for gold. Colorado was the land of the wild west!

Today Colorado still has gold. Only now it is not really gold. It is money, printed in Colorado by the United States government. People ski in the mountains in winter and hike in them in the summer. Colorado is called the Rocky Mountain state.

Near Rocky Mountain National Park.

Fast Facts

COLORADO

Capital and largest city
Denver (467,610 people)
Area
103,598 square miles
(268,318 sq km)
Population
3,307,912 people
Rank: 26th
Statehood
Aug. 1, 1876
(38th state admitted)
Principal rivers
Arkansas River,
Colorado River,
South Platte River
Highest point
Mount Elbert; 14,433 feet
(4,399 m)
Motto
Nil sine numine
(Nothing without providence)
Song
"Where the Columbines Grow"
Famous People
Frederick Bonfils, M.
Scott Carpenter,
Douglas Fairbanks,
Florence Rena Sabin,

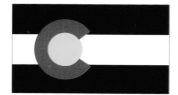

*S*tate Flag

*R*ocky Mountain
columbine

*L*ark bunting

*C*olorado Blue
spruce

About Colorado
The Centennial State

Detail area

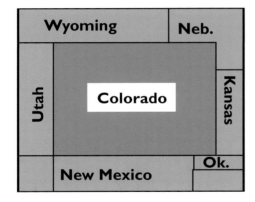

Colorado's abbreviation

Borders: west (Utah), north (Wyoming, Nebraska), east (Kansas, Nebraska), south (Oklahoma, New Mexico)

Nature's Treasures

Colorado has many minerals. In the 1800s, miners found gold and silver. In the 1900s, oil was found. Other minerals in Colorado are coal, **natural gas**, and building materials like gravel and stone.

Plants need minerals in the soil to grow. So Colorado also has good land for farming.

Colorado's many rivers and lakes provide lots of water. Water is hard to find in the western United States. So dams and tunnels bring water from Colorado to other parts of the west.

The weather is another treasure from Colorado. It is dry and warm much of the year. Many people visit Colorado to enjoy its weather.

Opposite page: The Colorado River.

Beginnings

Long before people existed, Colorado was part of the bottom of a giant ocean. This was the Ice Age. Dinosaurs walked the lands of Colorado!

Around 100 B.C., **Anasazi** Native Americans moved to the Colorado **Plateau**. Anasazi means "ancient ones." About 1100 years later, they began to build **pueblos** in the cliffs of the plateau. Pueblos are like big buildings with many small houses inside them.

In 1276 a long dry spell killed the crops. Other Native Americans attacked them. The Anasazi moved away. Around 1500, other Native Americans moved in. Ute, or "people of the blue sky," and Bannock settled in western Colorado. Apache, Comanche, Kiowa, Navajo, and Pawnee came to southern Colorado.

In the 1600s, Spanish and French explorers came to Colorado. In 1803, France sold its part of Colorado to the

United States. In 1848, the United States took another part from Mexico after winning the Mexican-American War.

In 1858 gold was discovered in the Colorado mountains! Many people came to look for gold and settle the land. In 1876, Colorado became the 38th state to join the United States.

In the late 1800s, railroads were built in Colorado. Then tunnels were built through its mountains. In the 1900s, **irrigation** projects and dams were built. Later, oil was discovered, which brought more new people.

In the 1990s the largest airport in America was built. Today, many people still come to Colorado. They no longer come for gold or oil. They come to ski on its mountains!

Mesa Verde National Park.

B.C. to 1500

The First Coloradans

 100 B.C.: The **Anasazi** move to the hills and valleys of the **plateau** area in western Colorado. Later they build **pueblos** in the cliffs.

 1276: Almost no rain for 23 years kills crops. The Anasazi move away.

 1500s: Ute and Bannock move into west Colorado. Apache, Comanche, Kiowa, Navajo, and Pawnee Native Americans move into southern Colorado. Arapaho and Cheyenne move to the plains in eastern Colorado.

Colorado
B.C. to 1500

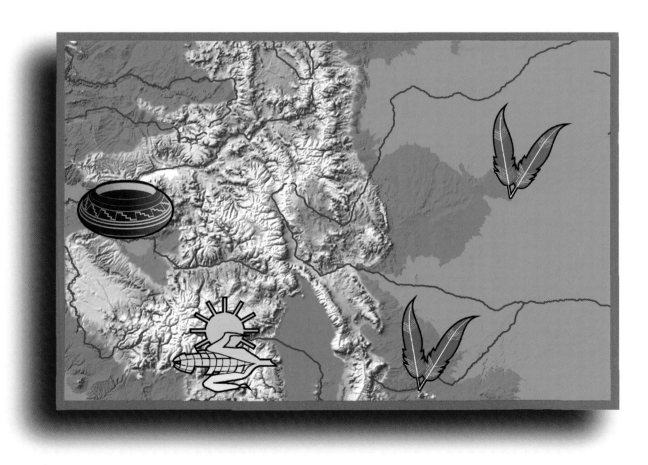

1500s to 1800s

New Arrivals

 1600s: The Spanish and French settle and trade with Native Americans in Colorado. The Native Americans begin hunting with horses.

 1803: France sells its land in Colorado to the U.S. Later, Mexico loses its land in Colorado to the U.S.

 1806: Zebulon Pike explores "Pike's Peak" mountain.

 1858: Gold is found. Miners and settlers move to Colorado from eastern United States.

Colorado

1500s to 1800s

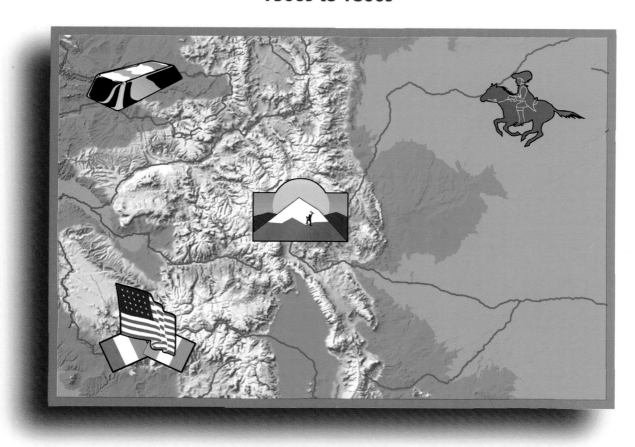

1800s to Present

Statehood to Today

1876: Colorado becomes the 38th state. Railroads are built in Colorado.

1900s: Oil is found in Colorado.

 1940s: New jobs grow, like building airplanes and working for the government. Tunnels are built through mountains.

 1960s: New **irrigation** and dam projects bring water to people throughout Colorado.

 1990s: The Denver International Airport opens.

16

Colorado

1800s to Present

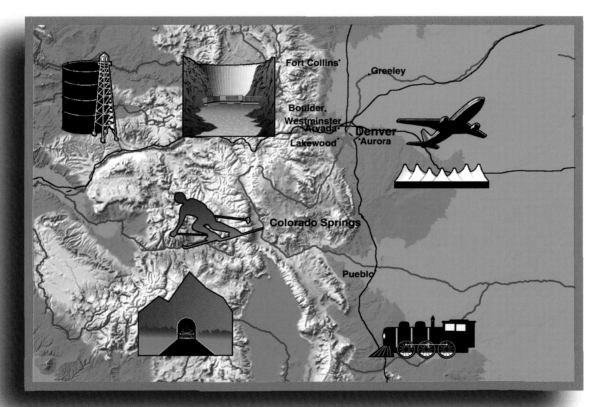

Colorado's People

There are more than 3.3 million people in Colorado. Most of them live in cities. Most of the cities are along the east side of the Rocky Mountains.

Many Coloradans are white. White people came from England, Germany, Italy, Russia, and other countries in Europe. Many Coloradans are Latinos. Latino people came from Central America and South America.

Other Coloradans are African American, Asian American, and Native American. Many Utes live in the Southern Ute **reservations**.

Kit Carson, a trapper in the Wild West, lived in Colorado. Jack Dempsey, one of the best boxers in history, came from Colorado. Molly Brown became rich mining silver in Colorado. She also helped keep many people from drowning when the ship Titanic sank. The movie *The Unsinkable Molly Brown* is about this famous Coloradan.

Frederico Pena was mayor of Denver until 1991. Then he was named by President Clinton to head an office in Washington, D.C. The singer John Denver named himself after the city he loves!

Kit Carson

John Denver

Jack Dempsey

Splendid Cities

The capital of Colorado is Denver. Denver also is the largest city in Colorado. And Denver was the first big city in the United States to grant women the right to vote!

Near Denver are cities called Aurora and Lakewood. South of Denver is Colorado Springs, the second largest city in Colorado. Pueblo is in southern Colorado.

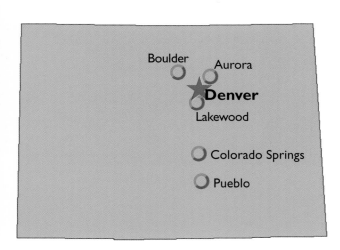

Boulder, Colorado, is the only city in the United States that gets water from a melting **glacier**. The water from the glacier supplies the whole town!

Denver, Colorado

Colorado's Land

Colorado is shaped like a big, square box. The west side is hilly, with valleys and **mesas**. The north part has hills and **plateaus**. The east side has plains. The middle of the state is filled with a **range** of mountains. This range, called the Rocky Mountain range, goes all the way from the border with Canada at the top of the United States to the border with Mexico at the bottom!

Many rivers and lakes carve waterfalls, canyons, and cliffs in Colorado's land.

The Royal Gorge canyon is more than 1,000 feet (300 meters) high. You and 250 of your friends would have to stand on each other's shoulders to reach the top! Lake Granby is 600 acres (240 hectares) and is Colorado's biggest lake.

Cactus and yucca grow in the dry parts of Colorado. Flowers like columbines and mountain lilies grow there too. Colorado's trees include cottonwood, spruce, pines, and firs.

Big animals of Colorado are elk, bears, and pronghorn. Small animals include prairie dogs, beavers, foxes, coyote, bobcats, and skunks.

Colorado is mostly dry and sunny. But in the mountains it can be cool. It snows and rains more in Colorado's western hills.

Elk in Rocky Mountain National Park.

Colorado at Play

The Denver Art Museum has many Native American art pieces. The Denver Broncos football team plays at Mile High Stadium. The Colorado Rockies joined Major League Baseball in 1993.

Tourists visit Colorado resorts and spas. Rodeos are also popular in Colorado. At rodeos, people ride and show trained horses. The Colorado State Fair has carnival rides, horse races, music, a rodeo, and more.

Many beautiful parks fill Colorado. Mesa Verde and Rocky Mountain are national parks. Other scenic places are Pikes Peak, the Royal Gorge canyon, and Dinosaur National Monument.

Opposite page: Skiing is a favorite sport in Colorado.

Colorado at Work

Most Coloradans used to work in the mines digging for gold and silver. Now only a few dig. They dig for coal, **natural gas**, and oil; and they use big machines to help them.

Ranching, farming, and **manufacturing** are other forms of work in Colorado.

Most people work in service. They cook and serve food, work in banks, and do many other things for tourists who visit the state or people who live there.

The biggest service area is in government. Many military bases and one of the biggest mints in the United States are in Colorado. A mint is where money is made!

Opposite page: U.S. Air Force Academy, Colorado Springs, Colorado.

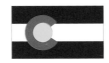

Fun Facts

•Colorado means "colored red" in Spanish. Colorado's mountains and rivers can look red. This is because water washes over the red clay and rocks in parts of the land.

•Colorado is called the roof of North America because it is so high. It also is called the tallest state. The highest point in Colorado is Mount Elbert. It is 14,433 feet (4,399 meters) tall.

•Colorado is the eighth largest state in the United States. It is 103,598 square miles (268,318 sq km).

•Colorado's nickname is the Centennial State. Centennial means 100. Colorado became a state 100 years after the United States of America became a new country.

•More rivers begin in Colorado than in any other state. The Continental Divide is a long line of mountains in

Colorado. All rivers west of the Continental Divide flow into the Pacific Ocean. All rivers east of the Continental Divide flow into the Atlantic Ocean.

•Colorado has the highest suspension bridge in the world. A suspension bridge hangs loose like a swing.

Royal Gorge suspension bridge.

Glossary

Anasazi: the name of a nation of Native Americans that lived in Colorado 2,000 years ago. Anasazi means "ancient ones."

Drought: long period of time with no rain or snow.

Glacier: large mass of frozen water.

Irrigation: to bring water from its source to another place, usually by digging ditches or using pipes.

Manufacture: to make things.

Mesa: high, flat-topped hill with steep sides.

Natural gas: a gas found in the earth that is used as a fuel.

Plateau: flat area that is higher than the land around it.

Pueblo: large dwelling built from bricks made of clay along the side of a cliff. Pueblos were built by the Anasazi. Many separate living spaces were in each pueblo. Many families lived inside a single pueblo.

Ranching: a large farm where ranchers raise animals, instead of growing plant crops.

Range: long line of mountains. The Rocky Mountain range contains the Rocky Mountains. It extends from the northern U.S. to the southern U.S.

Reservation: land set aside for Native Americans.

Internet Sites

Colorado Live Cams
http://www.geocities/Yosemite/3910/Imgcam.htm
More than thirty live photos from around the state. Best viewed during the day. Please be patient, this takes a few minutes to load. But it's well worth the wait.

The Colorado Web
http://www.rmi.net/colorado
Information and links on Colorado Cities, Businesses, Government, Counties, Parks, Skiing, Clubs, Education, Recreation, Sports, Weather, and Sights.

Online Colorado
http://olcolorado.com
Aims to present the "best sites of colorado" ...as quickly as possible!

These sites are subject to change. Go to your favorite search engine and type in Colorado for more sites.

PASS IT ON

Tell Others Something Special About Your State

To educate readers around the country, pass on interesting tips, places to see, history, and little unknown facts about the state you live in. We want to hear from you!

To get posted on ABDO & Daughters website E-mail us at "mystate@abdopub.com"

Index